MacDuff the MacDufficult

The Sixty-Pound Puppy

Martin Koeppel

Drawings by Nancy Walker

Cucciolo Grosso Press
(Big Puppy Press)

Published by Cucciolo Grosso Press/Inner Eye Publishing
P.O. Box 295
Fairfax, CA 94930

Pencil and pen and ink drawings by Nancy Walker
Cover design and restoration of pencil drawings by Nancy Marie
Book design by Nancy Marie, Martin Koeppel and Sandra Stamos
Mechanicals: Marie–Josée Studio, Mt. Shasta, CA
Copyediting by Sandra Stamos and Karla Maree

©2006 by Cucciolo Grosso Press (utilizing previously copyrighted, but not published, material 1988, 1997)
Printed in Canada by Friesens.
All rights reserved. No part of this book may be reproduced or transmitted, in any form or by any means, without prior permission in writing from the publisher.

Koeppel, Martin, 1938-
    MacDuff the macdufficult: the sixty pound puppy / by
Martin Koeppel.
   p. cm.
   ISBN 0-9660418-9-5

   1. Sheep dogs--Poetry. 2. Sheep dogs--Pictorial
works.   I. Title.

PS3611.O363M33 2005   811'.6
                                        QBI05-600123

An Oyvey Production

Printed on acid-free recycled paper with soy-based ink

This book is dedicated to MacDuff, an Old English Sheepdog who, if he could, would lie underneath the covers, his head on a pillow, just like anybody else.

It is also dedicated to Jake, Etienne, Eric, Alicia, Evan, Aaron, Frankie, Mondo, Colleen, Stephanie, Nick, Sydney, and Jonathan.

"Take this little shaggy one," said the Fairy Godmother, "and all your troubles will be over."

v

The No Picnic Table of Contents

Dubious Quote iv

THE SIXTY-POUND PUPPY...................1
A Puppy from Where? 2
The Puppy Digests
    The Dragons of Eden........................4
The Furball of Innocence 7
A Puppy's Lament 8
A Puppy's Hope......................................11
The Parade..12
The Puppy on a Roll..............................14
The Puppy At Work 17
In the Name of the Puppy. 18
The Puppy's Escape..............................20
The Puppy At Home 22
A Puppy's Greeting 24

Automotive Puppy 1	26
Automotive Puppy 2	28
Automotive Puppy At the Copy Shop	30
The Puppy and the Sea	32
A Puppy's Bedtime Snack	34
A Puppy's Quality Time	36
The Puppy At Rest (finally)	38

DREAMS OF MACDUFF	40
Mary Had a Little Lamb	41
Old King Cole	42
Sing a Song of Sixpence	44
Little Jack Horner	46
Little Miss Muffet	49
Jack and Jill	50

EPILOGUE	51
Questionable Blessing	52
Order Form for More Books	55

THE SIXTY-POUND PUPPY

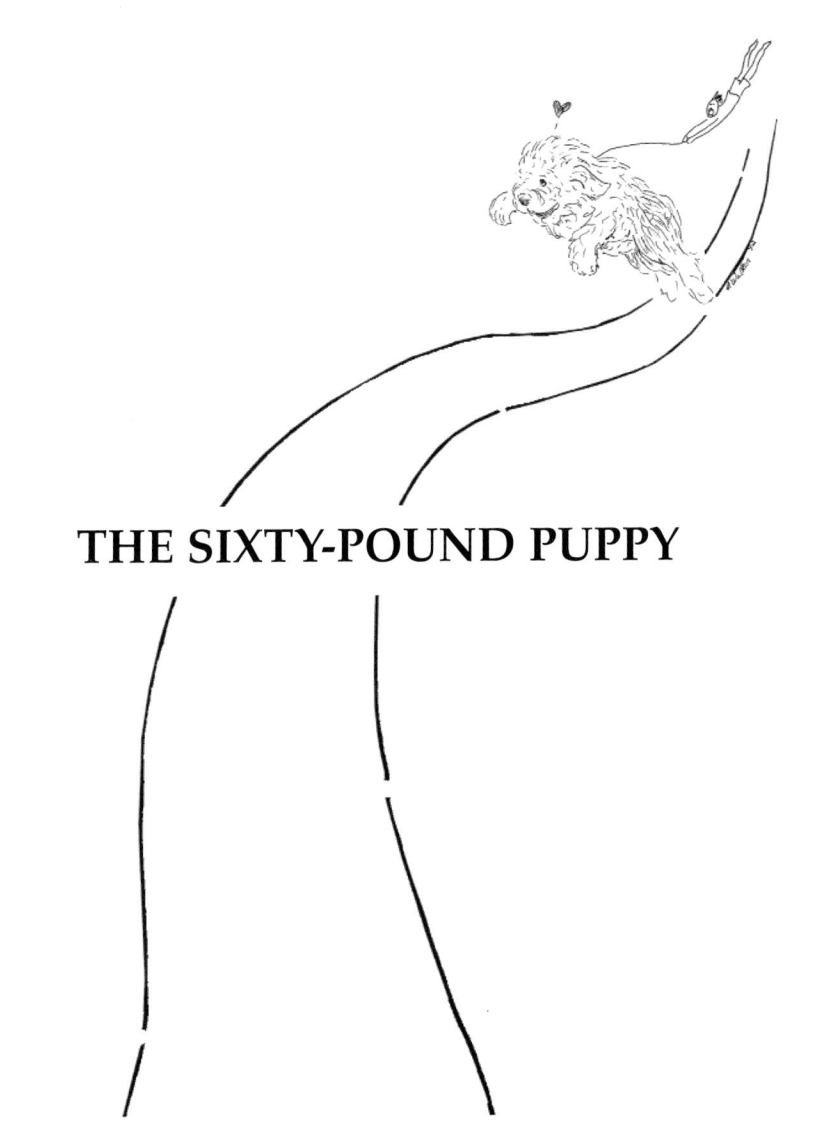

A Puppy From Where?

This is a puppy who is seven months old.
When we first got him we thought,
"I guess he'll be a medium-size dog."
But our vet took one look and said,
"This could be a colt instead of a pup."
At first he was about the size
of a small loaf of bread.
Now that's about the size of his head.
"Excuse me," people say, "but your dog
just jumped up and licked me on the lips."
Is this just a spell or is this really
THE PUPPY FROM HELL?!

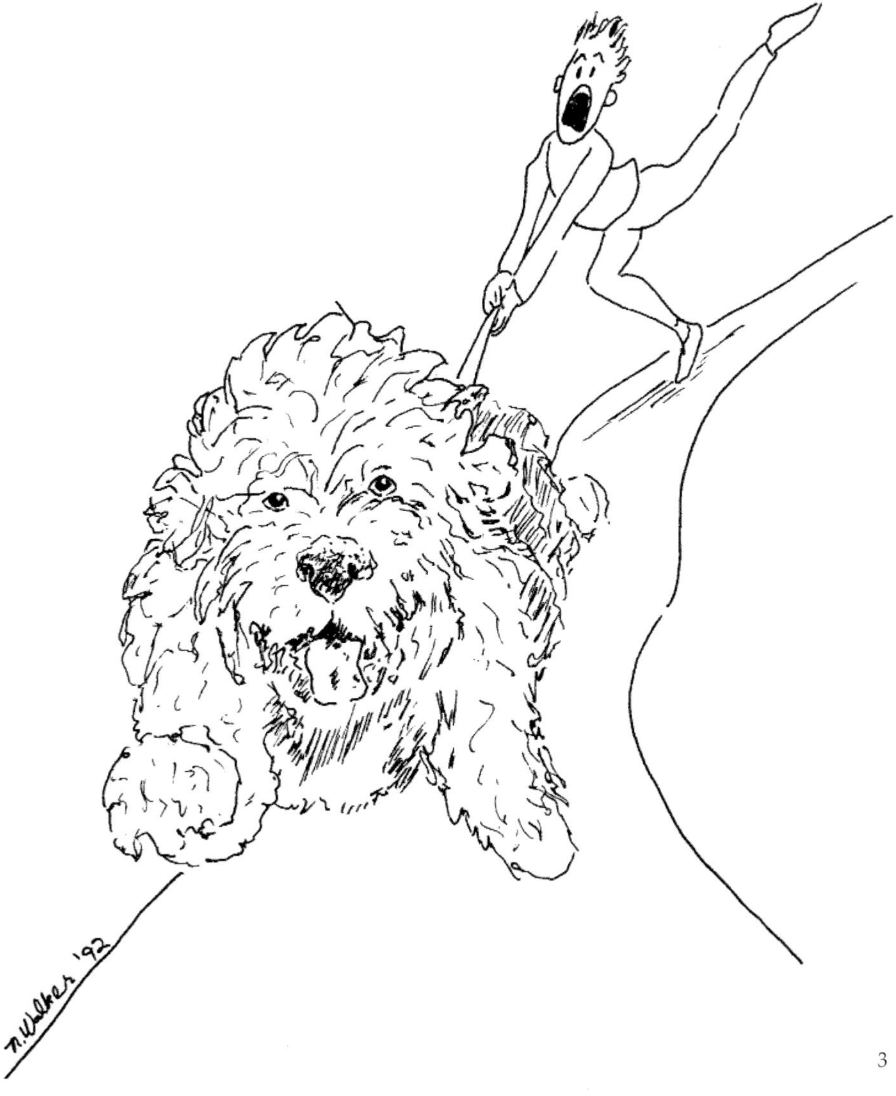
N. Walker '92

The Puppy Digests *The Dragons of Eden**

By eight A.M. he had eaten the dental floss
and thrown up on the rug, though I didn't know
until later when I felt it accidentally
with my foot. "Oh good," I said, "the puppy's up."

Remember those books you stacked on the floor?
Well, MacDuff just selected one for his maw.
It's *The Dragons of Eden*. What would
Carl Sagan say? Can it be possible?
Is this the PUPPY FROM ANOTHER PLANET?
Was there a rocket ship? Did he man it?

---

* A book about the nature of the universe by astronomer Carl Sagan.

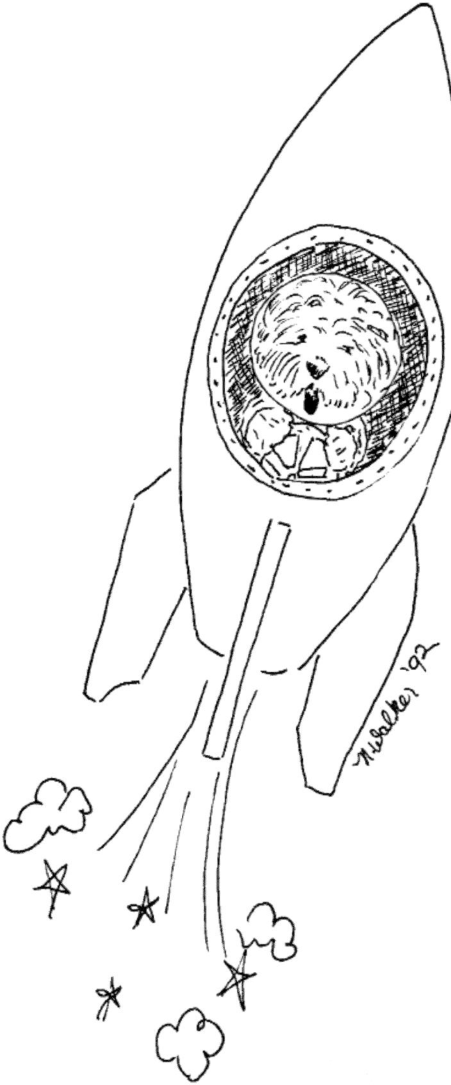

The Furball of Innocence

Loves to drink from the toilet bowl,
drips water on the seat,
leaves a trail of it to the door,
this mysterious visitor;
this is especially fun if you do not
look before you sit
or if your socks were too dry
before you walked across the floor.

A Puppy's Lament

Even though I scratch
at the door like fate itself,
my Mom doesn't want me in there.
She is typing my Dad's poems.

She knows I will empty
the half-open drawer of her underdrawers;
she knows I will steal a prize sock
and run away with it;
she knows I love to sink my teeth
into her playing cards.

How can she love me
and leave me like this
in the lonely hallway,
outside her warm light,
away from the tap, tap, tap
of fingers I would lick and chew—
wouldn't you?

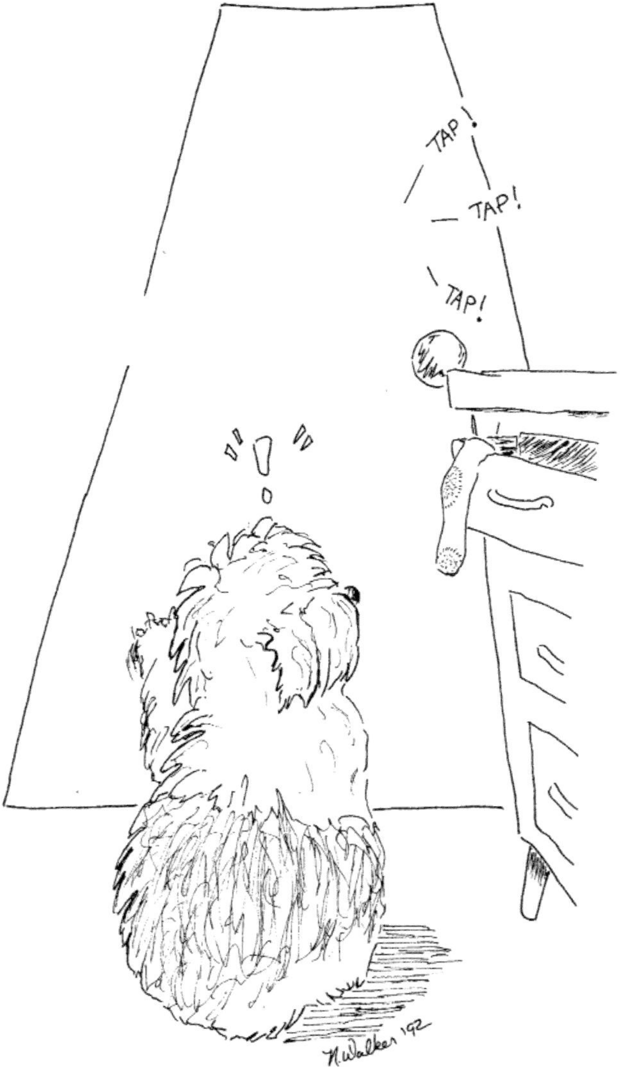
TAP!
TAP!
TAP!
N. Walker '92

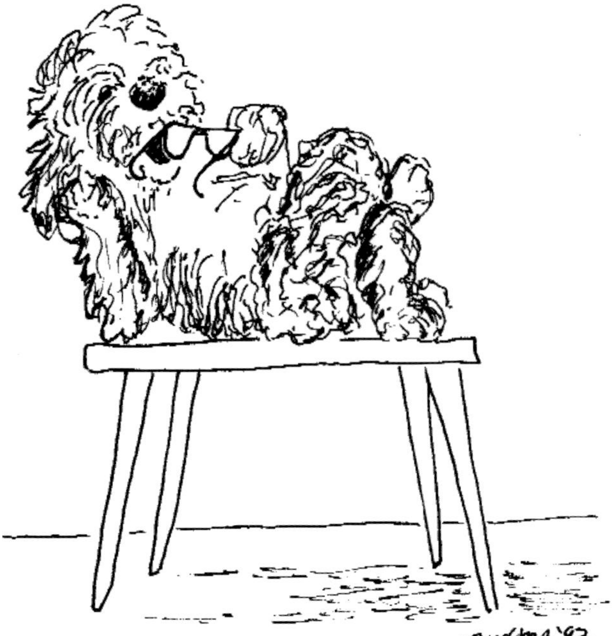

A Puppy's Hope

I am learning to climb.
Why are people so surprised
to find me on the kitchen table?

We puppies grow lots of new teeth.
If you remember—this hurts,
so it helps to chew on things:
plastic eyeglasses seem to
relieve the discomfort,
but sometimes the leg of a rocking chair
feels almost as good as a barbecued rib.

The Parade

I saw a man in a furry white suit
in the Fourth-of-July parade;
when I grow up I'm gonna look
just like him.

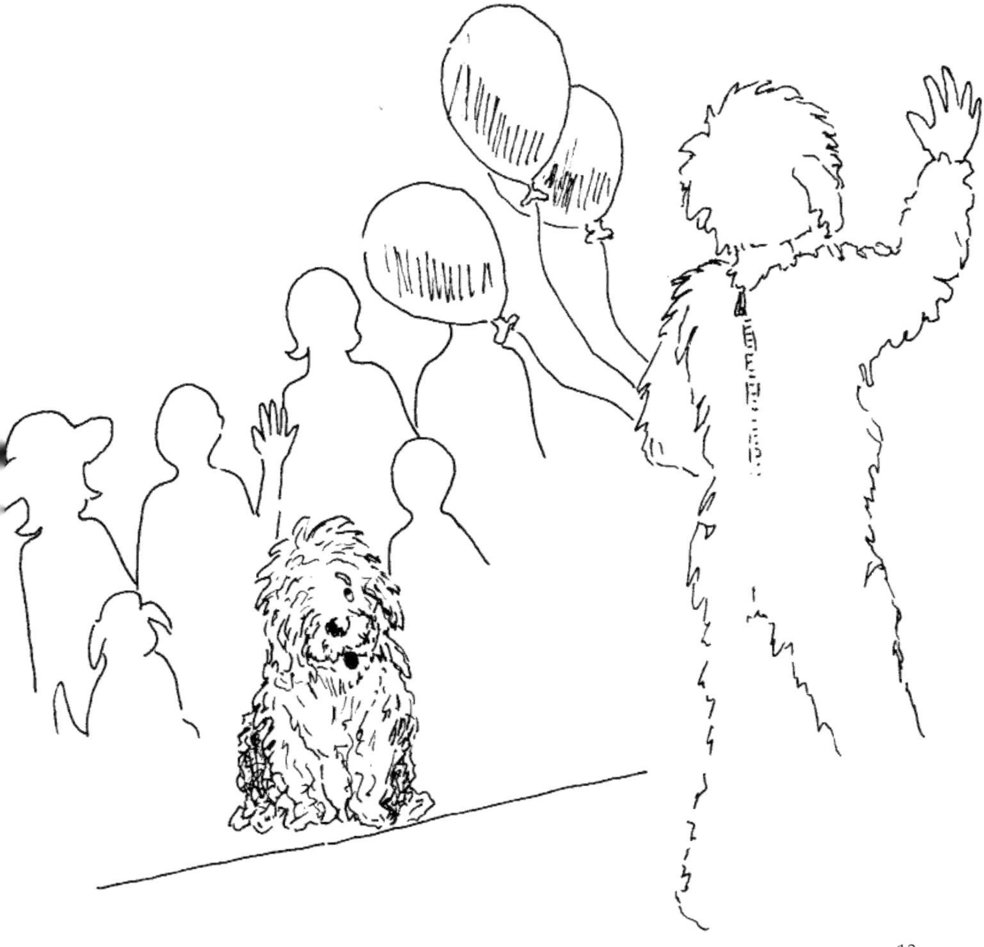

The Puppy on a Roll

This is a trouble-makin' dog
who follows me around;
just nipped my elbow,
take 'im to the pound.

Sing a song of sixpence,
he drinks like a swine.
If he keeps it up, he'll throw up;
what do you think we'll find?

Plastic and pipe stems
and parts of my glasses;
that's when I think of who sold
him to us and what she must have thought:
"Let's put this nut with those two asses."

You can tell I love him,
he's gotten under my skin;
with two huge puppy fangs,
should I turn him in?

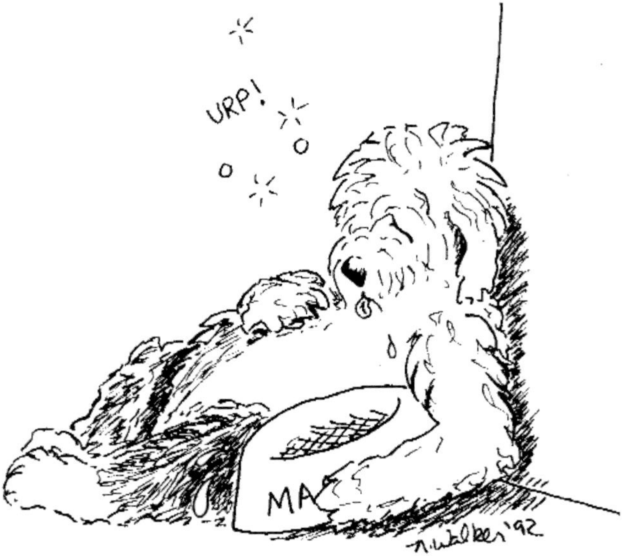
URP!
MA
N. Walker '92

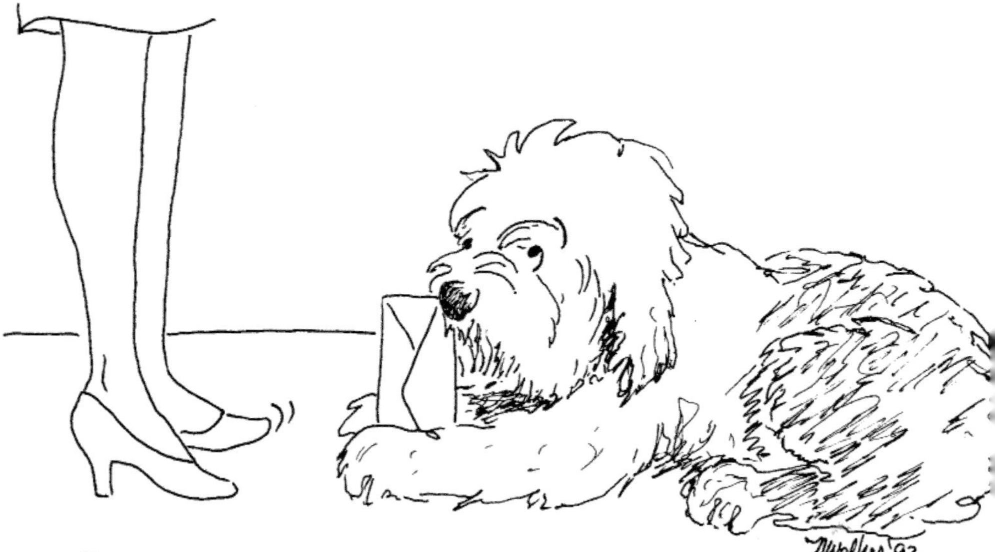
NWalker '92

The Puppy At Work

The sixty-pound puppy has just taken
his Mom's paycheck off the kitchen table.
Quick as she is, he is quicker
and she cannot catch him. If she tries
to ignore him he may bring it back.
She tries to ignore him. He sits just out of range,
on the floor nearby, the envelope between
his paws, opening one end with his teeth.
He must have carefully watched her
put the paycheck in its place.
This is what happens when you do not pay attention
to a patiently waiting puppy.

In the Name of the Puppy
    (wave a weak arm)

Today the little angel licked the turntable
of the phonograph, you know, to see how it moved.
Then he leaped up to say, "I love you" to the grocery-
lady but she and the sixty-pound puppy were OK,
because their fall was broken by two large bags of food.

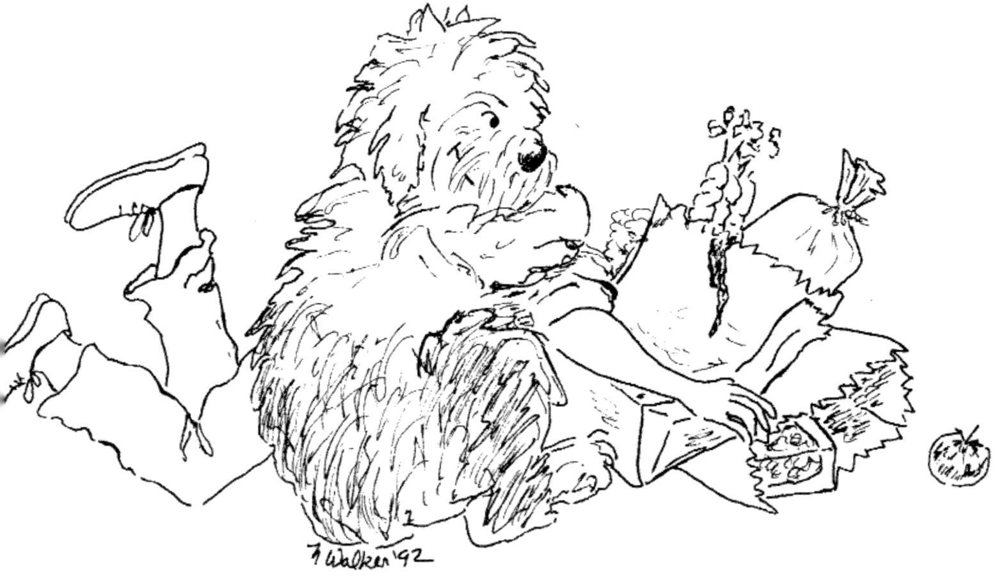

The Puppy's Escape

Late for work, I forgot to lock the back door.
The puppy does not seem to enjoy solitude,
the peaceful silence of an empty house.
He has learned that sufficient force applied
by his big black nose can open a sliding-glass door.

Driving like a hot streak down the street,
I imagine I hear a galloping noise.
Suddenly I am not in California at all
but in wild Africa, on the plains of the Serengeti,
only to look out the window and see that the galloping noise
is MacDuff running alongside the car,
keeping up easily, smiling at me,
happy to be finally on our way.

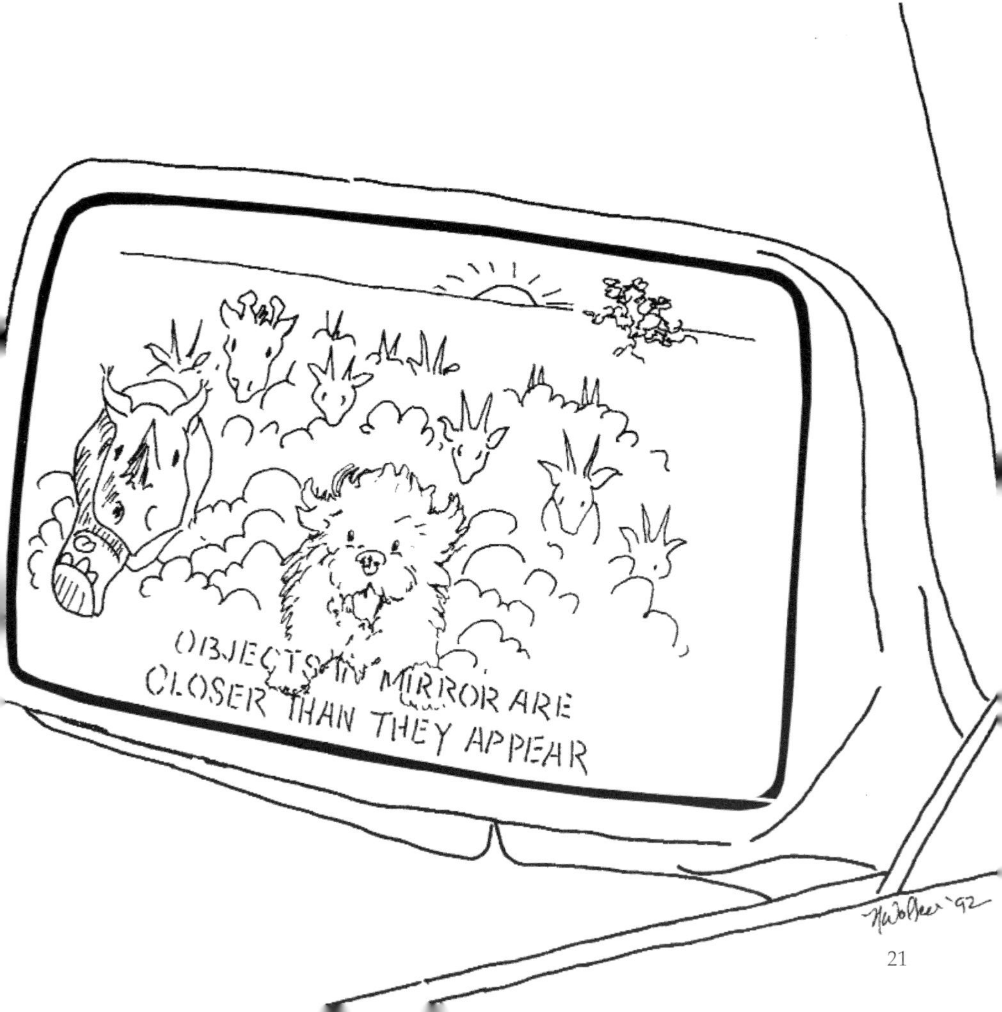
OBJECTS IN MIRROR ARE
CLOSER THAN THEY APPEAR

The Puppy At Home
      ("can't he be kept outside?")

Today I forgot to take the little darlin'
with me to the grocery store when I went.
When I got back he had chewed up a wastebasket
I thought would sit in the bathroom forever.

The basket was once made up of long leaves
of wild grass. He took it from the bathroom,
which must have been too small, to the living room,
which must have been too clean and just didn't have
that old puppy feeling.

Then he added the shreds of a large black and
yellow ad from the mail. Now he is chewing on
that bone you left out this morning so he wouldn't
get bored.

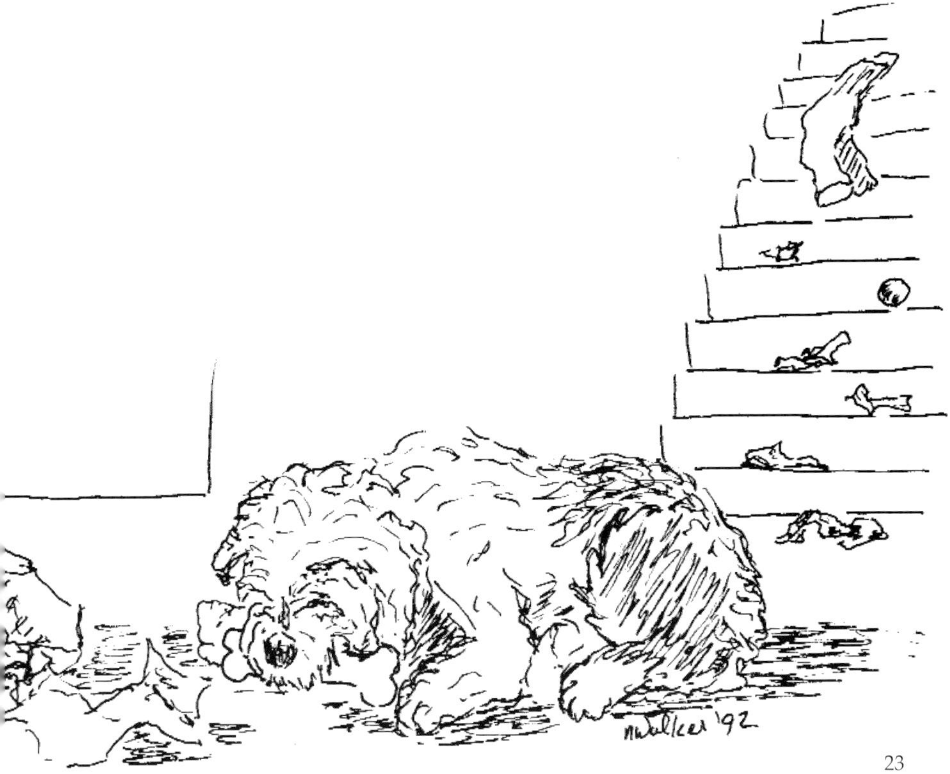
MWalker '92

A Puppy's Greeting

It is impossible to kneel before the stereo
without a flurry of fur blurring my vision.
I have stooped to his level; it must be time
to play. And there is something about my coming
through the front gate that necessitates a leap.

I am tired of his leaping. Although he has learned
not to knock you down, people who do not know
him tend to think a large flying animal may not
bode well for them, especially near their heads.
They don't think, "Oh, it's just a sixty-pound
puppy saying, 'I love you'."

Unscathed, except for a friendly "hello" nip or a kiss,
they seem relieved and grateful. Their fortunes are good.
They have met the dragon. They have conquered
each other.

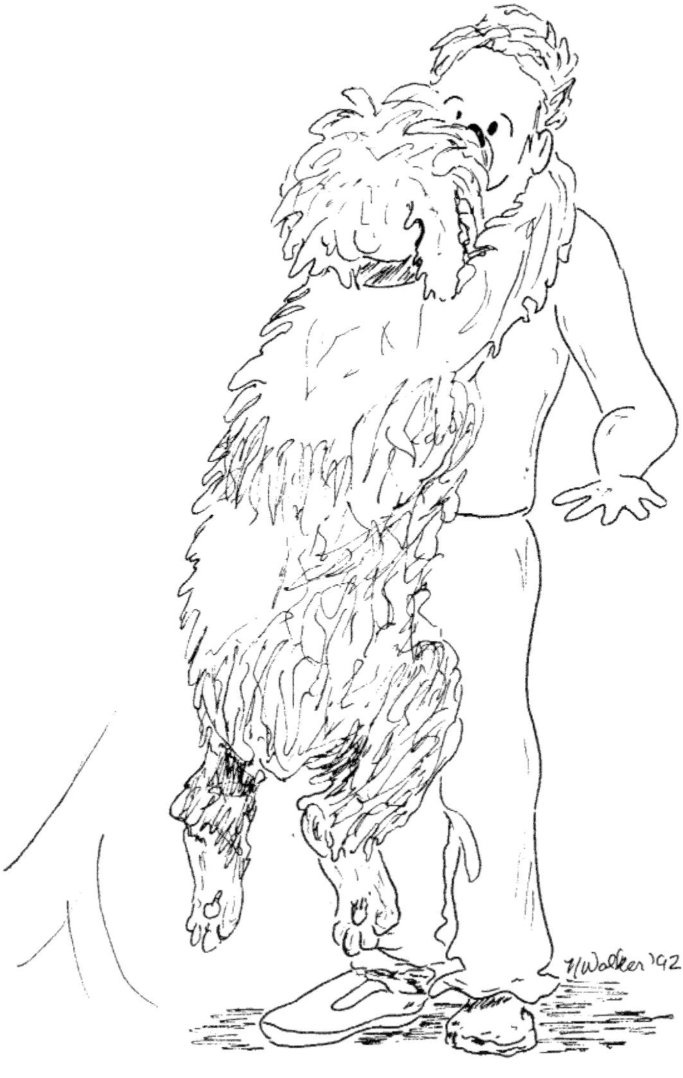
NWalker '92

Automotive Puppy 1

Likes to kiss me when I'm driving,
tries to climb into my seat.

Automotive Puppy 2

Once he jumped out the window,
(we were driving by a baseball game).
"My puppy just leaped from a speeding car,"
was what I thought. But he was running
towards left field, not crumpled
in the street.

Now we keep the windows up a bit,
just in case he sees a team
he thinks he has to meet.

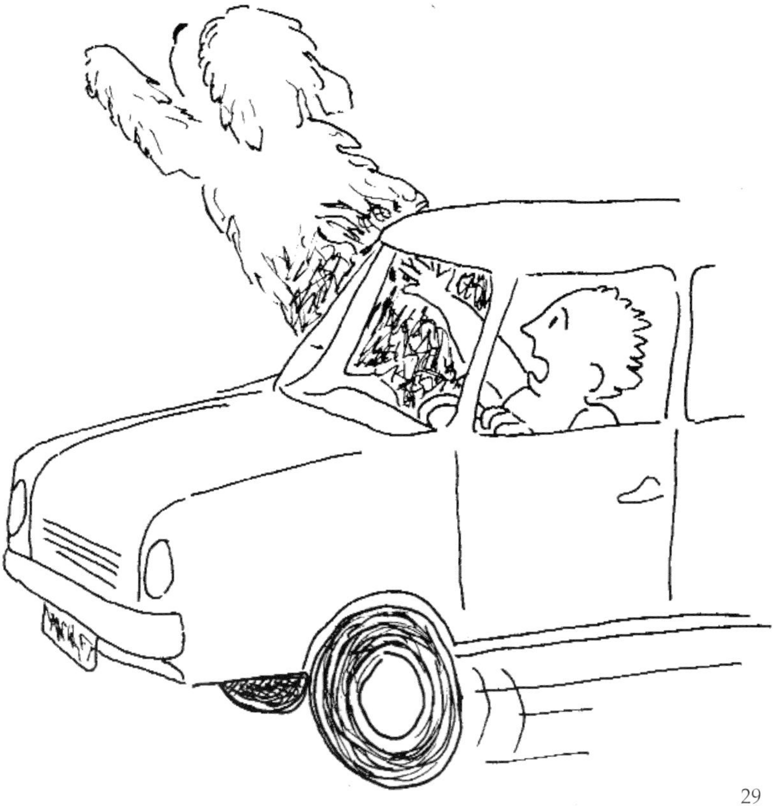

Automotive Puppy At the Copy Shop

Left alone in the car, MacDuff heaves
himself at the windows and barks.
I try to ignore this.

His bounding around releases
the emergency brake and the car
rolls into the street, blocking traffic.
Someone yells, "Look, a dog is driving!"

Meanwhile, I was blithely making copies.
I look out the window;
MacDuff and the car are gone!
"Someone has stolen them," I cry.

Outside, MacDuff and the car are
surrounded by irate drivers, the police,
a tow truck, and a beautiful, tough-looking
woman named Sadie, the tow-truck lady.
She growls at me in a raspy voice,
"Is this your car or what?"

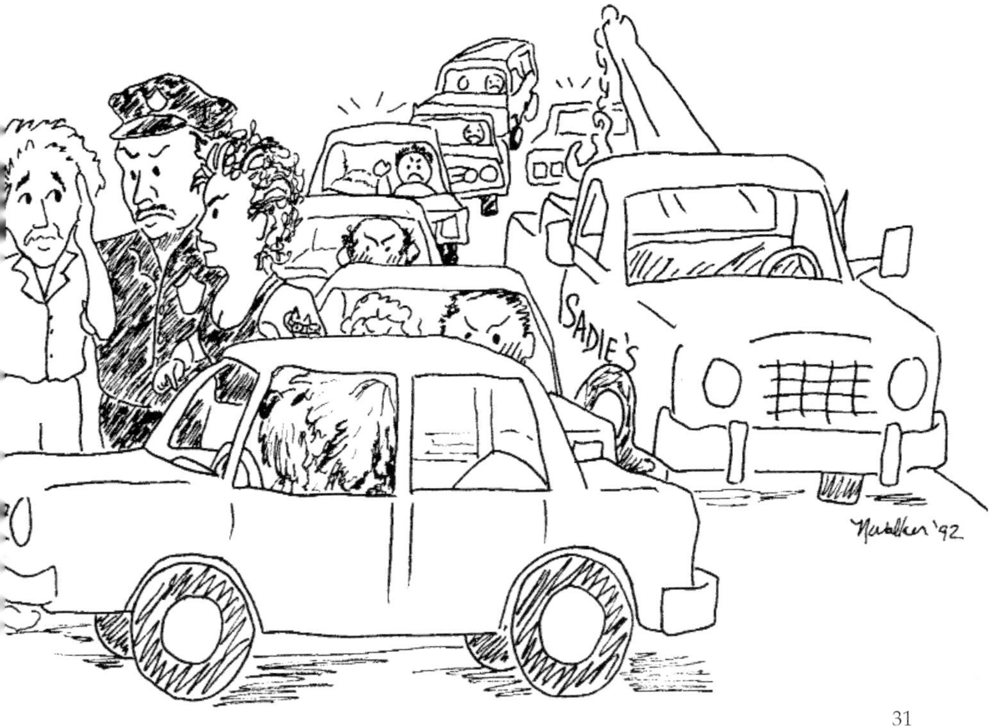
SADIE'S

The Puppy and the Sea

Remember the black and gold geese
that were napkin rings? One went the way
of your lipstick but it looked a bit
like driftwood swept up on a wave of green rug.

Here, nothing is safe from being at least mouthed,
so I try to remember to close doors, store everything
up high, learn to recognize the sounds of things
I thought I owned make in his teeth.

He likes to make waves in the water bowl with his paw,
the waves in my stomach sickening as I watch the floor–
washed only this morning–begin to resemble the Dead Sea.

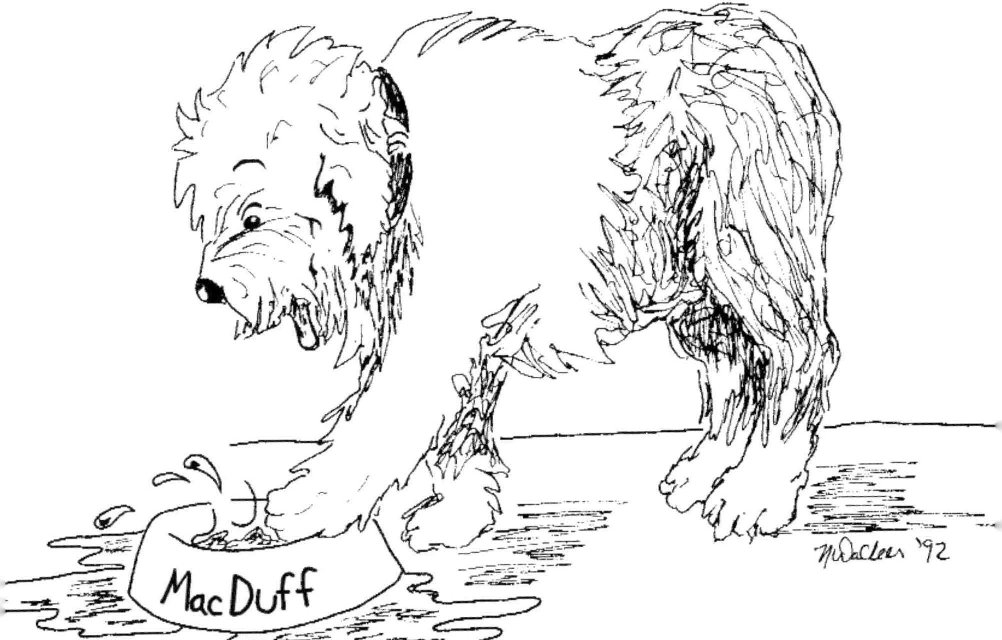
MacDuff

A Puppy's Bedtime Snack

He likes to lick out the yogurt cup
after it is discarded,
then with loud cracks and gnashes,
he eats the cup itself.

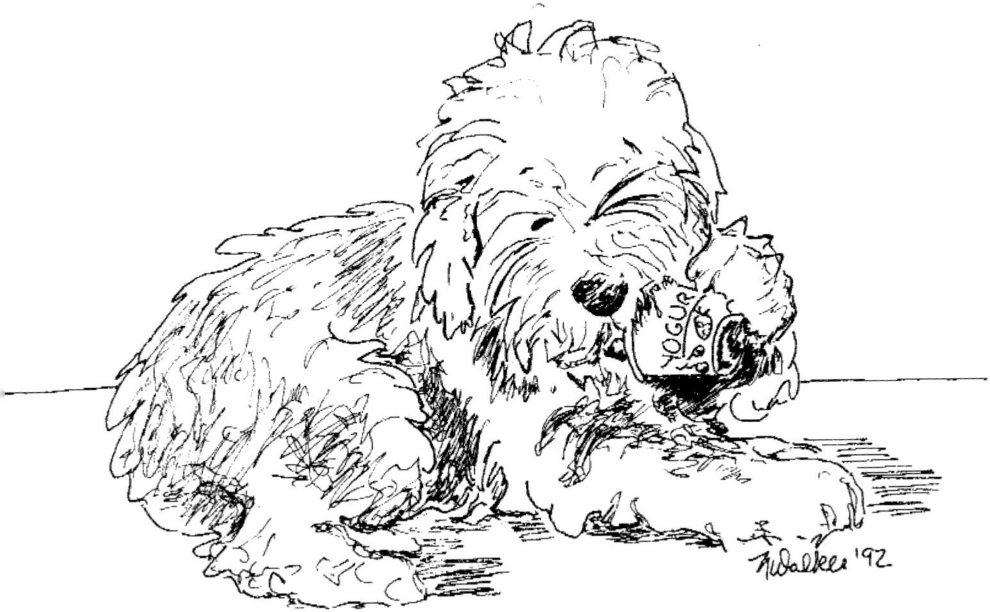
YOGURT
Walker '92

A Puppy's Quality Time

I tried to explain to MacDuff that he had two fathers,
a human father and a fuzz-butt father;
that his fuzz-butt father whom he resembled,
lived back East and did things like
parade in dog shows and chomp on bones;
that I, his human father was raising him
and that I was tired and going to bed.

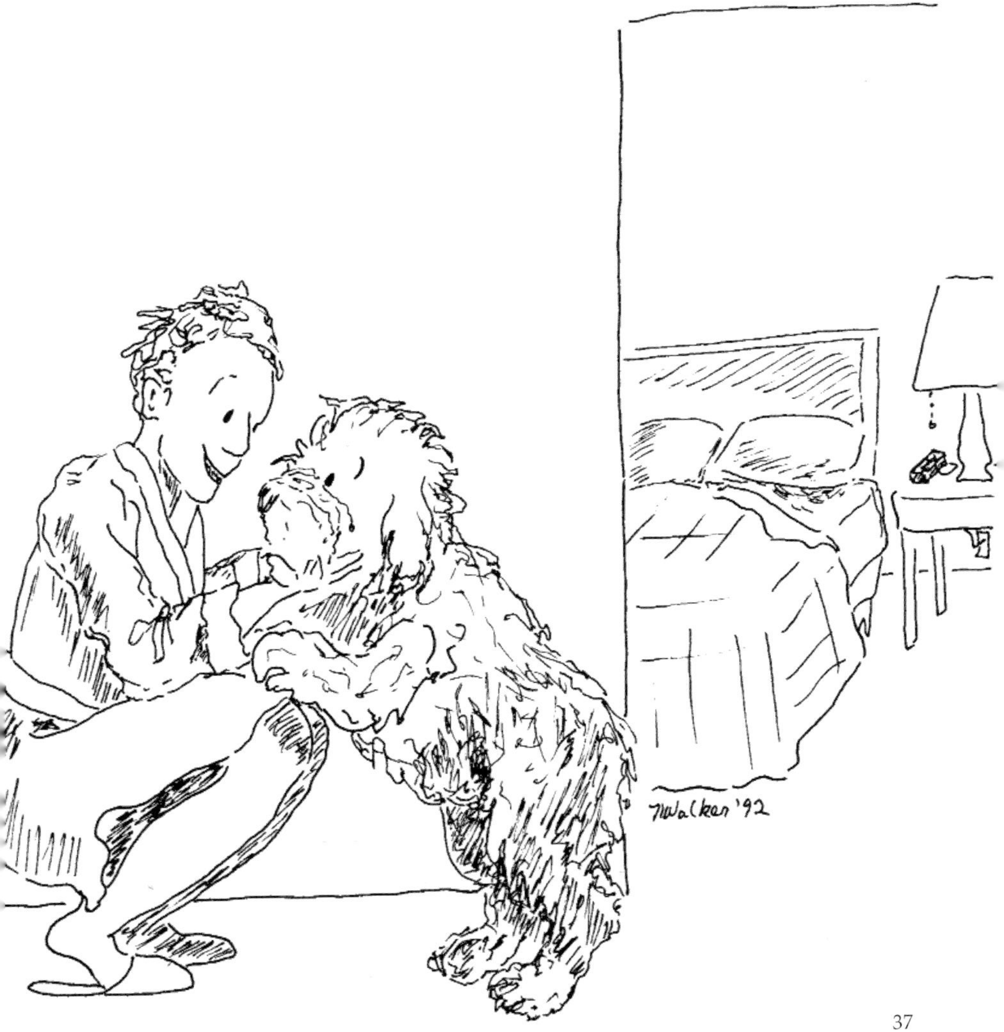
NWalker '92

The Puppy At Rest
    (finally)

Now I lay me down to sleep
A dog of trouble
And of sheep.

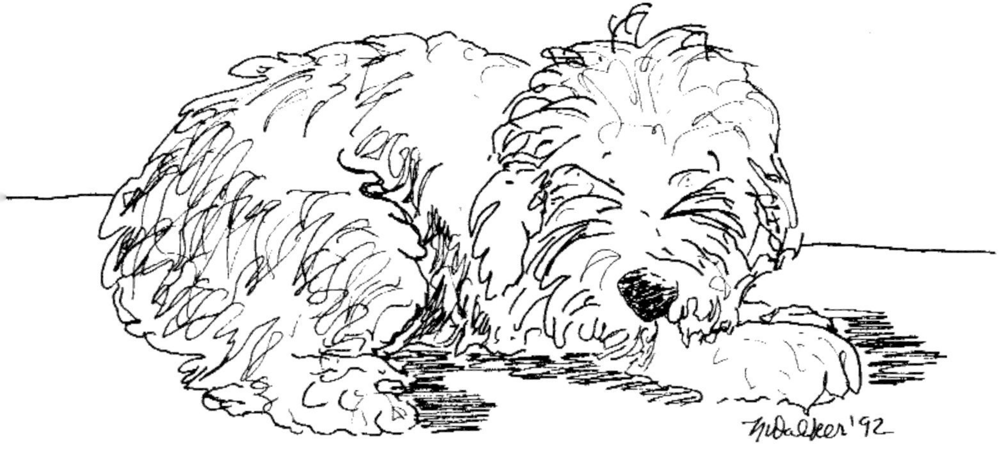

DREAMS OF MACDUFF

In the following dream-rhymes, MacDuff invades Mother Gooseland. Whereas the tales in the *Sixty-Pound Puppy* are all based on truth, these are purely (and gratefully) imaginary. Any resemblance to persons living or dead is purely coincidental.

Mary Had a Little Lamb

Mary had a little lamb,
its fleece was white as snow;
and everywhere that Mary went
the lamb was sure to go.

The lamb was herded by MacDuff.
They followed her to school,
but 'cause it was against the rule
the teacher made her take them home.

And so they moseyed on their own…
got busted…to the pound….
Then we had to bail them out!

Old King Cole

Old King Cole
was a merry old soul,
a merry old soul was he.
He called for his pipe
and he called for his stole
and he called for his fiddlers three.

He didn't call for MacDuff
But MacDuff came up
and peed on his rug
and stole his stole
(and the king got a cold)
and he stole his pipe
and he hid it under a tree.

And that's why the king
went back to cigarettes
though we know it's no good
for his heart!

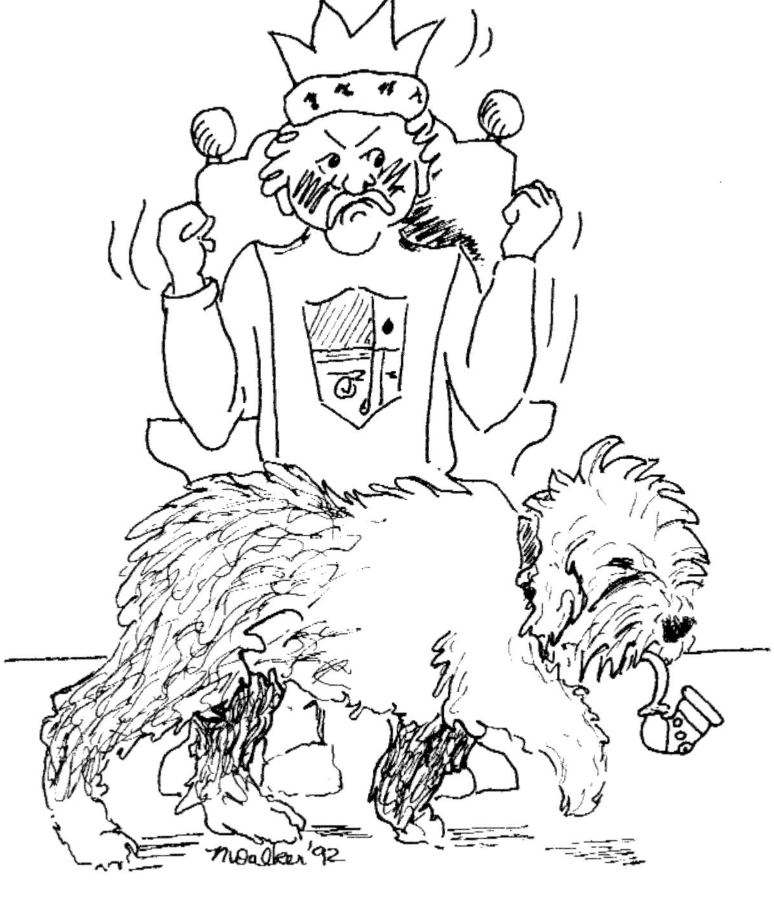

Sing a Song of Sixpence

…the king was in his counting house
counting out his money.
The queen was in the parlor
eating bread and honey.
Four-and-twenty blackbirds
were baked in a pie.
That's a lot of bird poop…
"You guys are going to
have to find a place of your own,
we have enough of a mess with MacDuff."

"Besides," we said, "No More Pets!"

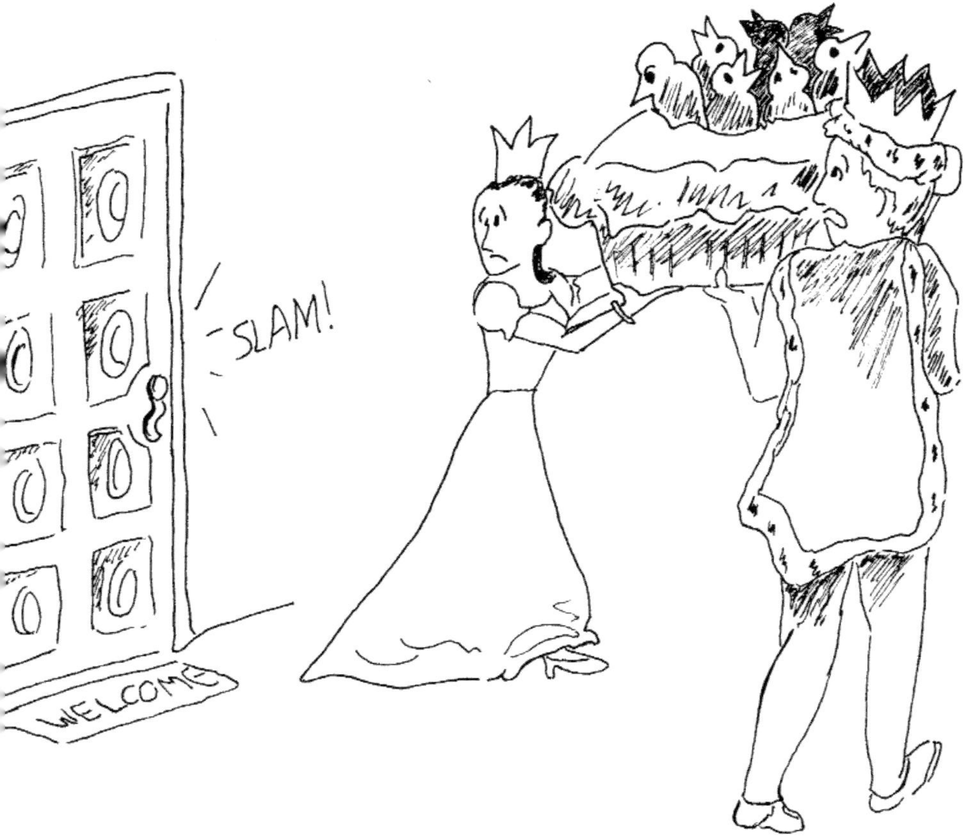
SLAM!
WELCOME

Little Jack Horner

Little Jack Horner
sat in his corner
eating his Christmas Pie.
He stuck in his thumb
and pulled out a plum
and said, "Oh, what
a good boy am I."

But then MacDuff
stuck in his nose
and pulled out a pair
of plum-flavored hose.
"These socks taste great,"
he said to Jack,
"what happened to their toes?"

47

48

Little Miss Muffet

Little Miss Muffet
sat on her tuffet
eating her curds and whey.
Along came a spider
who sat down beside her…

Then along came MacDuffet
who sat on the spider
and Miss Muffet said,
"Where did you hide her?"

"And by the way,
what happened to Jack;
what did you say?
He was doin' so good
since he started A.A."

Jack and Jill

Jack and Jill went up the hill
to fetch a pail of water.
Jack fell down and broke his crown
and Jill came tumbling after.

MacDuff ran up the hill sure 'nuff.
Jill sprang to action; sent him back
all the way to town to get
paramedic help for Jack!

EPILOGUE

The slumbering puppy awakens.
He gets up at the crack of dawn
and runs rapidly around the house
for at least half an hour.

May the puppy
of enlightenment
sit on your foot!

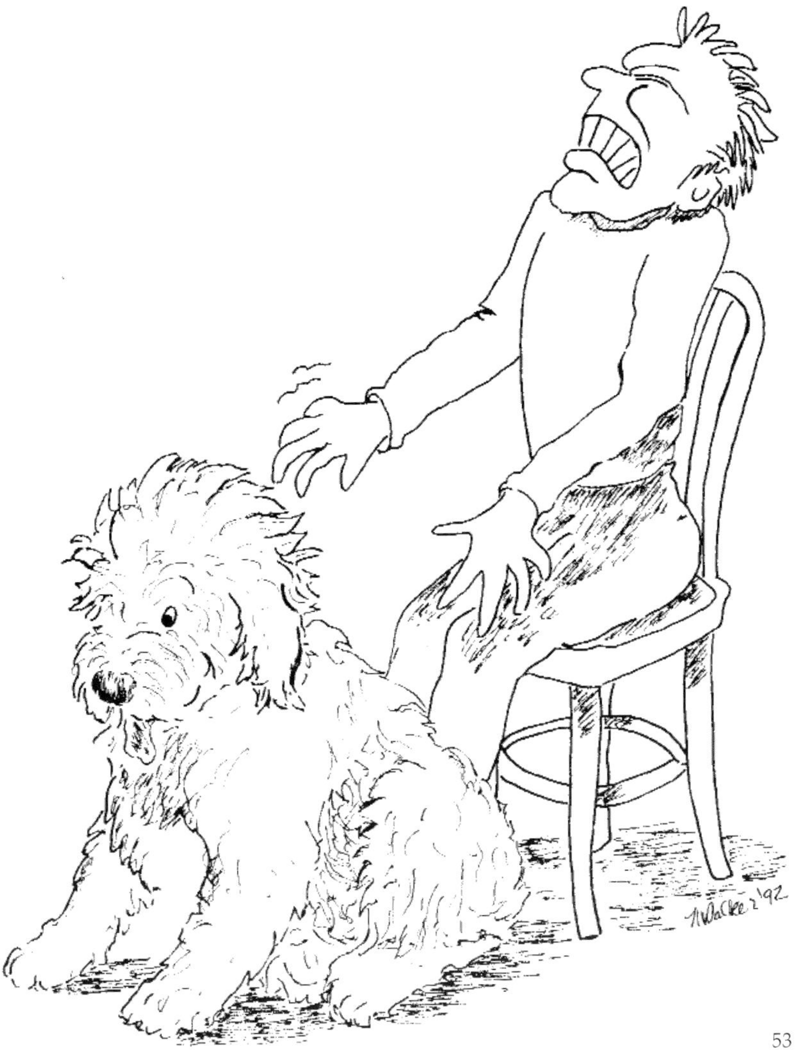

The Order Form for More Books

call us at **1-415-459-6343**

or

copy and mail the order form below to:

Cucciolo Grosso Press, Box 295, Fairfax, Ca 94930 *(Please print)*

www.bigpuppypress.com

Name: _____ e-mail address: _____

Mailing Address: _____

City, State, Zip: _____ Daytime phone: _____

Quantity	Title	Price	Total
	MacDuff the MacDufficult	$14.95	
	Womansmith (Love Poems by M. Koeppel)	$14.95	
	CA residents ADD 7.75% Tax		
	Shipping for first book (outside USA please call)	$4.00	
	Shipping for each additional book	$1.50	
	TOTAL DUE		

☐ Check/ Money Order   ☐ Visa/MasterCard

Card Number: _____ Expiration Date: _____

Name on the card: _____ Signature: _____

woof!